END TIME
PROPHECY
(Part One)
(Revised Edition)

REV. DR. FRED OPOKU-GYIMAH
(D:D., D.Th, D.Min., Ph.D.)

⊛IBUNET
Publishing

Published by
Cibunet Publishing
Email: admin@cibunet.com
Website: www.cibunet.com

Dedication

This book is dedicated to God: the Father, Son and the Holy Ghost who opened my life to the End Time prophecy.

Acknowledgement

Special thanks to my wife Margaret Opoku-Gyimah popularly known as "AUNTIE MAGGIE" you are what any man would wish for. Thank you for being there all the time,; My deepest appreciation to Mr. Christian and Justina Udaze for their kindness; sincere thanks to Ishola Akinbowale, Pastor, Faith Life Ministries and Evangelist Philip Duah; Mr. Kofi Nyankomah, principal Accountant, Ghana Broadcasting Corporation, Accra; Mother L. Eady, my Godmother; Rev. Mamie Raji, my Pastor, and all of Bethel Holy Church of Deliverance, Manhattan, New York, for your encouraging supports.

Content

<u>Chapters</u>

Foreword 1

When a book of this nature is being presented, purpose, intent and sound biblical basis must be put to consideration.

In dealing with topics relating to the "ENDTIME" we have seen inadequacies in the knowledge and understanding of how and when it will take place.

However, we must not ignore this subject entirely but remain fixed in the word of God because therein is security, stability and truth.

Apostle Fred Opoku-Gyimah is a faithful and humble servant of God, and a man of integrity. I have benefited much through fellowshipping and sharing the things of God together with him. The purpose of this book is to equip the Body of Christ with the in-depth knowledge and understanding of the signs of the end time.

This book has been written and released through much prayer and God given instruction. The truth emphasized herein has shed more light on the subject.

The Bible instructed, study to show thyself approved... in order to rightly divide the word of truth (2 timothy 2:15).

May this book serve in advancing the kingdom of God through you - the Reader. May you become strengthened by the power of the Holy Spirit, and may you be blessed abundantly in the precious Name of Jesus. Amen.

Rev. Ishola Akinbowale

Faith Life Ministries Bronx,
New York..

FOREWORD 2

The rise of environmental challenges, economic meltdowns and acts of terrorism that plaque our society today is the quest for answers about the era in which we live I, as it relates to end time biblical revelations.

While most principles of scripture that relates to daily living, family well-being, healing, deliverance and spiritual development are easy to understand, it requires unusual depths of insight to unveil end-time prophecies. Most people totally avoid reading the books of Daniel and Revelation that focus on the eschatology because they are unable to fathom the prophetic signs that are used to characterize the end-time. The privilege of working with Dr.Opoku-Gyimah on the publication of this book and find his understanding of this subject very intriguing. Clearly he is an authority on the subject and has done due diligence in communicating in a very concise manner how end-time prophecy can be understood in the light of today's realities

I encourage everyone to read this book and reserve a copy in your personal library.

(Kenneth Walley is the Senior Pastor of New Faith Tabernacle & Chairman of Cibunet Corporation).

CHAPTER ONE

DANIEL'S SEVENTIETH WEEK AND THE TRIBULATION

As a prelude to Daniel's Seventy Weeks and The Tribulation, I wish to start with the revelation and interpretation of King Nebuchadnezzar's vision and revival of the Roman Empire. I believe this will properly prepare you for the above subject.

The Revelation And Interpretation Of Nebuchadnezzar's Vision Of Earth's Governments

Daniel explained the dream saying:

Your Majesty, in your vision, you saw standing before you a giant STATUE, bright and shining, and terrifying to look at.

Its head was made of the finest gold; its chest and arms were made of silver; its waist and hips of bronze; its legs of iron; and its feet partly of iron and partly of clay.

While you were looking at it, a great stone broke loose from a cliff without anyone touching it, struck the iron and clay feet of the statue, and shattered them.

At once the iron, clay, bronze, silver, and gold crumbled and became like the dust on the threshing-place in summer. The wind carried it all away, leaving not a trace. But the stone grew to be a mountain that covered the whole earth." *Daniel 2:31-35 (Good News Bible)*

Daniel told the King: This is the dream. Now I will tell Your Majesty the meaning."

Your Majesty, you are the greatest of all Kings. The God of heaven has made you emperor (Kingdom}, and given you power, might, and honor. He has made you ruler of all the inhabited earth and ruler over all the animals and birds. You are the head of gold. After you there will be another empire, not as great as yours (empire of silver}, and after that a third, an empire of bronze, which will rule the whole earth. And then, there will be a fourth empire, as strong as iron, which shatters and breaks everything. And just as iron shatters everything, it will shatter and crush all the earlier empires. You also saw that the feet and the toes were partly clay and partly iron. This means that it will be a divided empire. It will have something of the strength of iron, because there was iron mixed with clay. That means a part of the empire will be strong and a part weak.

The iron which was mixed with the clay also means that the rulers of that empire will try to unite their families by intermarriage. (This division is represented in the ten toes of the statue. The clay element mixed with the iron in the feet represents the mixture of Church and State). But they will not be able, just as iron cannot mix with clay Daniel 2:36-43 (Good News Bible).

Daniel went on to say,

At the time of those rulers the God of heaven will establish a Kingdom that will never end. It will never be conquered, but will completely destroy all those empires and last forever.

Daniel said, that is why you saw how a stone

broke loose from a cliff without anyone touching it and how it struck the statue made of iron, bronze, clay, silver, and gold" Daniel 2:44-45 (Good News Bible) And this was the meaning of the vision of the King interpreted by Daniel in the second year that Nebuchadnezzar was King.

The Time Of The Gentiles

The great giant statue as interpreted by Daniel, symbolizes the entire period known in prophecy as the time of the Gentiles or the future course of world empires until the end of this age.

The giant statue Composed of four different metals:

- The head of **GOLD**
- The chest of **SILVER**
- The thighs of **BRONZE**
- The legs of **IRON** (An feet of both iron and

clay).

NEBUCHARDNEZZAR'S STATUE

It is extremely important to know which empires these metals represent.

As Daniel Chapter Two points out, the head of gold represents the BABYLONIAN EMPIRE, which was led by Nebuchadnezzar himself.

The second empire, represented by the chest and arms of silver, stands for M4EDIAPERSIA or MEDO-PERSIAN EMPIRE established by Cyrus.

The third empire represented by the belly and thighs of bronze symbolizes the GREEK or GRECIAN EMPIRE which was established by Alexander the Great.

Finally, the legs and feet of both iron and clay represent the fourth empire, which was the ROMAN EMPIRE, led by Claudius. This empire will rule until the Second Coming of the Lord, when He shall establish his eternal Stone Kingdom (Daniel 7:13-14)

The Roman Empire endured longer than its predecessors. In fact, the Roman Empire still continues, as represented in the Nations of Europe. Because the first three empires had passed away, the fourth empire, which is, Roman Empire held universal sway.

Even at the time of the Lord Jesus birth, Dr. Luke recorded that Emperor Augustus then Emperor of the Roman Empire ordered a census to be taken throughout the Roman Empire (Luke 2.1).

As Daniel said, all the empires were man made. They were formed by the power and authority of man and have controlled and is still controlling.

The Loose Stone

But Daniel interpreted the dream that, a stone broke loose and came to destroy the whole statue. The most intriguing thing about that stone was that, no hand was holding or controlling the stone.

This means that God's Kingdom will come to control or to destroy all other Kingdoms.

In fact, when you study the Bible, you will know that the end of the Roman Empire is nigh and

God's Kingdom is at hand to fulfill this prophecy.

Because the devil is not happy with the coming of the Kingdom of God, over the years, he has used some ambitious men like Napoleon Bonaparte, Frederich Barbarosa, Adolf Hitler and some other great men of the world to attempt to replace the Roman Empire or build a fifth world Empire, but each of them failed.

Daniel stated in his interpretation that, the stone cut out of the mountain without hands, which smites and scatters the clay, iron, bronze, silver and gold (symbolizing the World Powers), is the true Church, the Kingdom of God.

I am happy to let you know that the true Church, the Kingdom of God, the Stone Kingdom, is being formed during this gospel age. It is not by might, nor by power, but by the Spirit of God.

From Stone To Mountain

Notice that the stone did not become the mountain until it has smitten and destroyed the statue. So that the universal Church in the full sense, becomes the Kingdom to fill the whole earth but only after the day of wrath upon the nations, that is, Daniel's Seventieth Week.

Who formed the Stone Kingdom? They are those who do not follow the evil teachings of the devil and have not learnt what others call, the deep secrets of Satan.

These are those who have accepted Christ as their personal Savior; those who win the victory and continue to serve and worship the Lord to the end.

Revelation 2:26-28 says; "To those who win the victory, who continue to the end to do 'what I want, I will give the same authority over the nations, to rule them with an iron rod and to break them to pieces like clay pots. I will also give them the morning star."

As I said before, some great men of the past have attempted to build a fifth World Empire but they failed. This was because Nebuchadnezzar's vision predicted that no world empire would ever successfully replace the Roman Empire

Two Legs And Ten Toes

At the moment the Roman Empire is divided into Eastern and Western Empires. The two legs of the statue" signify this division, which started under Emperor Diocletian. The Eastern and Western Empires are going to enjoy a last-day revival in a ten Kingdom or a ten-nation group - the ten toes of the statue(Daniel2:40-4:3).

This revival is going to be political and in the form of states of dictatorships (iron) and democracies (clay). The secular world is already predicting some sort of a United States of Europe. The importance of this from a prophetic stand point is that, this is a major step in end-time events leading up to the Second Coming of Christ

CHAPTER TWO

DANIEL'S FOUR BEAST VISION: THE PREDICTED REVIVAL OF THE ROMAN EMPIRE

Several years later, and in the first year of Belshazzar, King of Babylon, Daniel himself had a parallel vision of this final stage of the revived Roman Empire which he describes one vision after another.

Now, let us look at the same four universal empires of the earth from the stand point of God and those in harmony with him, as portrayed in vision to the beloved prophet, Daniel.

Daniel's Vision

"'I saw in my vision by night, and behold, the four winds of the heavens (Political and Social Agitations) were stirring up the great sea (The Nations of the world).

And four great beasts came up out of the sea in succession, and different from one another.

The first (The Babylonian Empire under Nebuchadnezzar) was like a lion and had eagle's wings. I looked till the wings of it were plucked, and it was lifted up from the earth and made to stand upon two feet as a man, and a man's heart was given to it (Daniel 2:37, 38).

And behold a bear, (The Medes Persian Empire) and it raised up itself on one side (one dominion) and three ribs were in its mouth between its teeth; and it was told. 'Arise, devour more flesh.'

After this I looked, and behold, another (the Grecian Empire of Alexander the Great), like a leopard which had four wings of a bird on its back. The beast had also four heads (Alexander's generals, his successors), and dominion was given to it (Daniel 2:39; 8:20-22).

After this I saw in the night visions, and behold, a fourth beast (The Roman Empire) terrible, powerful and dreadful, and exceedingly strong.

And it had great iron teeth; it devoured and crushed and trampled what was left with its feet. And it was different from all the beasts that came before it, and it had ten horns, (symbolizing ten Kings Dan. 2:40-43; 7:23).

I considered the horns, and behold, there came up among them another horn, a little one, before which three of the first horns were plucked up by the roots; and behold, in this horn were eyes like the eyes of a man and a mouth speaking great things. *Daniel 7:2-8.*

The 1st BEAST- The Babylonian Empire

The 2ND BEAST- The Medes/Persian Kingdom

The 3RD BEAST - The Grecian Empire

The 4TH BEAST - The Roman Empire

CHAPTER THREE

THE VISION OF THE SEVENTY WEEKS

"Seventy Weeks (of years, or 490 years) decreed upon your people and upon your HOLY CITY (Jerusalem), to finish and put an end to transgression, to seal up and make full the measure of sin, to purge away and make expiation and reconciliation for sin, to bring in everlasting righteousness (permanent moral and spiritual rectitude in every area and relation) to seal up vision and prophecy and prophet and to anoint a Holy of Holies.

Know therefore and understand that from the going forth of the commandment to restore and build Jerusalem until (the coming of) the

Anointed One, a Prince, shall be seven weeks (of years) and sixty• two weeks (of years); it shall be built again with (city) square and moat, but in troublesome times.

And after the sixty-two weeks (of years) shall the Anointed One be cut off or killed and shall have nothing (and no one) belonging to (and defending) Him. And the people of the (other) prince who will come will destroy the city and the sanctuary. Its end shall come with a flood and even to the end there shall be war, and desolations are decreed. (Isa. 53:7-9; Nah. 1:8; Matt. 24:6- 14).

And he shall enter into a strong and firm covenant with the many for one week (seven years). And in the midst of the week he shall cause the sacrifice and offering to cease (for the remaining three and one-half years); and upon the wing or pinnacle of abominations (shall come) one who makes desolate, until the

full determined end is poured out on the
desolator." Daniel 9:24-27.

Interpretation

This Vision of the SEVENTY WEEKS foretold to
the precise day, discloses an important fact that
the SEVENTY WEEKS only cover the period
when the Jews are dwelling in their own land. It
is an unusual prophecy because the time
element is given so specifically and clearly. This
important revelation is not only an
interpretation of Prophetic Chronology, but it
is the key that unlocks the scriptures of
truth. This important revelation does not cover
the present period of their dispersion, but takes
up their history again when they return to their
own land. Thus covering the time from the
going forth of the decree to restore and rebuild
Jerusalem until the Second Coming of Christ

where He is going to set up His everlasting Kingdom. This revelation received by Daniel was one of the most amazing visions ever given to man.

Seventy Weeks

The expression SEVENTY WEEKS literally means SEVENTY SEVENS OF YEARS. The whole period of seventy sevens (70 times7) is 490 years which are determined or marked off apart from all other years. We are told in Daniel 9:24 that the purpose of the seventy weeks in six events.

- To Finish The Transgression.
- To Make An End of Sin.
- To Make Reconciliation For Iniquity.
- To Bring In Everlasting Righteousness.
- To Seal Up the Vision and Prophecy.
- To Anoint the Most Holy.

To Finish The Transgression

First of all, what is the meaning of TRANSGRESSION? It is the breach of law or duty; sin or revolt; rebel against lawful authority. We are told in Daniel 9:24 that this transgression has nothing to do 'with the Gentiles or the Church, but is in reference to the Jews (Daniel's People), and Jerusalem (The Holy City). Therefore this is the transgression of Israel in her rebellion against God. They failed to receive the Messiah and were broken off through unbelief from God's favor as a nation. Israel's transgression is not yet finished because they are still in disfavor with God. This will not end until Israel as a Nation repents and turns to God.

To Make An End To Sin

The concept of ending sin, leads to forgiveness and restoration and the beginning of a new spiritual plateau. The Bible says in Romans 21: 26-27;

"And so all Israel shall be saved: as it is written, there shall come out of Zion the Deliverer, and shall turn away ungodliness from Jacob: For this is my covenant unto them, when I shall take away their sin."

To Make Recommendation For Iniquity

Atonement for sin was made on the cross for the whole world but Israel, as a nation has not yet appropriated its benefits. This promise of reconciliation for iniquity undoubtedly refers to the death of Christ, "which is the basis of God's grace."

This end of sins will not be made until after the tribulation. From that time Israel will obey God for ever.

It is written in Isaiah 53:6; "... The Lord has laid on Him the iniquity of us all." But this has nothing to do with the .Jews as a people in this divine arrangement and administration of the affairs of the world.

If a Jew 'wants to get saved by the Blood of Jesus Christ, he must take away his 'religious nationality' and become a member of the Church (the body of Christ), in 'which, there is neither Jew nor Greek, slave nor free, male nor female, for you are all one in Christ Jesus" (Galatians 3:28).

But to purge Israel of their rejection of the Messiah, and accept them, Ezekiel 20:33, 34 says; "As I live, says the Lord God, surely with a mighty hand and an outstretched arm and with wrath poured out will I be King over you. And I will bring you out from the peoples and will gather you out of the countries in which you are scattered, 'with a mighty hand and an outstretched arm and with wrath poured out." (Also Zechariah 13:8, 9).

To Bring In Everlasting Righteousness

When the transgression of Israel has been finished, and their sins sealed up, and they have realized the full benefits of the atonement, then shall the Lord make a new covenant with the House of Israel. "The days are coming, declares the Lord, when I will raise up to David a righteous Branch, a King who will reign wisely and do what is just and right in the land. In his days Judah will be saved and Israel will live in safety.

This is the name by which he will be called: THE LORD OUR RIGHTEOUSNES (JEHOVAH TSIDKENU)." (Jeremiah 23:6; 33:16)

To Seal Up The Vision And Prophecy

There will be a time to seal up the vision and prophecy concerning Israel and Jerusalem. At that time, the transgression of Israel will cease. This will happen when Christ Himself returns in His visible presence on earth. At that time no additional vision or prophecy will be necessary.

To Anoint The Most Holy

Some Christians associate the MOST HOLY to

Jesus Christ. But the MOST HOLY here is never used for a person, and the Jew's will never associate this place with their Messiah. The

MOST HOLY is a place and not a person. It refers to the MOST HOLY place of the Millennial Temple. (Ezekiel 41:3-4).

One of the purposes of Ezekiel's Temple was to provide a dwelling place for the Divine Glory. Ezekiel sees the return of the Divine Glory to take up residence in the Temple's HOLY OF HOLIES during the Kingdom Age, as he saw its departure before the fall of the City (Jerusalem).

This is the place of His throne and the place of the sole of His feet, where He will dwell in the midst of the people of Israel forever (Ezekiel 43:1-7).

CHAPTER FOUR

THE SEVEN-YEAR COVENANT

According to Daniel, there will be a covenant between the Antichrist and Israel in the last seven years of Daniel's vision of the SEVENTY WEEKS of years. Daniel 9:27 revealed the seven years preceding the Second Coming of Christ will begin when a covenant is made with Israel by the Antichrist the leader of the ten-nation revived Roman Empire.

"And he shall confirm the covenant with many for one week and in the midst of the week he shall cause the sacrifice and oblation (offering) to cease, and for the ever spreading of abominations he shall make it desolate, even until the consummation, and the determined shall be poured upon the desolate" *Daniel 9:27.*

Who Is The "He" Daniel Was Talking About?

Some people think that the pronoun "HE" in Daniel 9:27 talks about or refers to the Messiah and that the covenant is the New Covenant that Christ proclaimed when he instituted the Lord's Supper. "For this is my blood of the New Testament, which is shed for many for the remission of sins," (Note *New Testament* refers to the *New Covenant*) *Matthew 26:28*

This New Covenant is different from the Seven-Year Covenant. The difference is that

Christ's New Covenant is an everlasting covenant. "God has raised from death our Lord Jesus, who is the Great Shepherd of the sheep, as the result of his sacrificial death, by which the ETERNAL COVENANT is sealed" *Hebrews 13:20.*

However, this Seven-Year Covenant will be broken at the end of three and a half years or in the midst of the Week (7 years). This is why the pronoun "HE" cannot refer to Christ but the Antichrist who is the Prince or the ruler that shall come.

Lesser And Greater Tribulation

This Seven-Year Covenant will be divided into two. The **Lesser Tribulation**- Three and a half years - and the **Greater Tribulation**- Another three and a half years. The covenant will be: fulfilled during the first half and he will have absolute power over all the nations of the earth and over those who will receive Christ by then. The second half will also last for only three and a half years (1260 days); "He will speak against the Supreme God and oppress God's people. He will try to change their religious laws and festivals, and God's people will be under his power for Three and a Half Years" *Daniel 7:25 (Good News Bible).*

The beast was allowed to make proud claims which were insulting to God and it was permitted to have authority for forty-two months" *Revelation* 13:5 *(Good News Bible).*

The Jews have thirty days for every month so forty-two months would come to one thousand two hundred and sixty (1260) days.

The First Half Of The Tribulation Week: [Daniel 9:27; Revelation 6 -13:18)

Daniel's vision on the Seventieth Week is not different from John's vision on the Tribulation Week. In the Lesser Tribulation, which will be for three and a half years, these are the things which shall be hereafter. The day of tribulation begins with the opening of the SEVEN SEALS (Revelation 6 - 8:6).

THE FIRST SEAL: The Coming Of The Antichrist On A White Horse

"And I saw when the Lamb opened one of the seals, and I heard, as it were the noise of thunder, one of the four beasts saying, come and see. And I saw, and behold a white horse: and he that sat on him had a bow; and a crown was given unto him: and he went forth conquering, and to conquer" *Revelation 6:1, 2.*

The rider on this white horse is the Antichrist and not Christ and it symbolizes the beginning of the reign of Antichrist. Don't confuse the white horse here with that of Revelation 19:11. Because this one is symbolical, while that of Revelation 19: 11 is literal. The **bow** and crown symbolize his great conquests. The rider cannot be Christ because, it is Christ who is opening the seal.

The First Horse

THE SECOND SEAL: **War**

"And when He had opened the second seal, I heard the second beast say, Come and see. And there went out another horse that was red: and power was given to him that sat thereon to take peace from the earth, and that they should kill one another: and there was given unto him a great sword" *Revelation 6:3, 4*

Red is the appropriate color for war and bloodshed. The sword is another symbol of war and bloodshed. The rider is pictured as having a great sword with which to take peace from the earth. 'This means men will slay each other (Daniel 9:6, 7).

The Second Horse

The Third Seal: **Famine**

"And when he had opened the third seal, I heard the third beast say, Come and see. And I beheld, and lo a black horse; and he that sat on him had a pair of balances in his hand. And I heard a voice in the midst of the four beasts say, A measure of wheat for a penny, and three measures of barley for a penny; and see thou hurt not the oil and the wine" *Revelation* 6:5, 6.

The color Black accompany gloom and

mourning. The rider of the black horse had a pair of **balances** - scales in his hand. This means food would be scarce, and sold by weight -a symbol of famine. A measure of wheat signifies scarcity of food, (Ezekiel 4: 10-47). And three quarts of wheat was thus three times more expensive than barley (the ratio of two to one was ordinary). The oil and wine need no cultivation but they -will run out too, because of the scarcity of food (Matt. 24:7).

THE*FOURTH SEAL:* **Death And Hell**

"And when he had opened the fourth seal, I heard the voice of the fourth beast say, come and see. And I looked, and behold a pale horse: and his name: that sat on him was Death, and Hell followed with him. And power was given unto them over the fourth part of the earth, to kill with sword, and with hunger, and with death, and with the beasts of the earth" Revelation 6:7, 8

The rider on the Pale horse represents pestilence and is called Death. The rampage of Death and/ Hell will be over the fourth art of the earth. This will come as a result of the riders of the first three seals.

The Fourth Horse

THE FIFTH SEAL: **Martyrdom**

And when He had opened the fifth seal, I saw under the altar the souls of them that were slain for the word of God, and for the testimony which they held. And they cried with a loud voice, saying, how long, O Lord, holy and true, doesn't thou not judge and avenge our blood on them that dwell on the earth?

And white robes were given unto everyone of them; and it was said unto them that they should rest yet for a little season, until their fellow servants also and their brethren, that should be killed as they were, should be fulfilled" Revelation 6:9-11.

The new Unger's Bible Dictionary gives the meaning of the word martyr as one who has proved the strength and genuineness of his faith in Christ by undergoing a violent death. The souls under the alter represent martyrs of the first half of the Seven -Year Covenant -- The lesser tribulation.

These are some of the Tribulation Saints who were saved after the Rapture of the Church. That is why their Blood cries for vengeance. The white robes represent righteousness and holiness and again it indicates the redemption of their souls. The martyrs were told to rest for a little season and wait until their fellow believer's who are to be slain during the greater tribulation period on earth shares the martyrdom (Revelation. 20:4).

THE SIXTH SEAL: **Anarchy**

And I beheld when he opened the sixth seal, and! Lo,, there was a great earthquake; and the sun became black as sackcloth of hair, and the moon became as blood; And the stars of heaven fell unto the earth, even as a fig tree casteth her untimely figs, when she is shaken of a mighty wind. And the heaven departed as a scroll when it is rolled together; and every mountain and island were moved out of their places. And the kings of the earth, and the great men, and the rich men, and the chief captains, and the mighty men, and every bondmen, and every freed men, hid themselves yes in the dens and, in the rocks of the mountains; And said to the mountains and rocks, Fall on us, and hide us from the face of him that sittteth on the throne, and from the wrath of

the Lamb: For the great *day* of His wrath is come; and who shall be able to stand?" *Revelation* 6:12-17.

This seal symbolizes governmental anarchy or social chaos. That is, the complete break up of society .Under this seal is revealed for the first time, God's intention to reveal His great wrath and judgment upon the persecutors. These are seven events under the sixth seal:

1. The Great EarthQuake: There are several earthquakes in the Bible but this is described as a great earth quake .There has been never such an earth quake like this one since the creation of man.

2. The Sun Became Black As Sackcloth Of Hair: The earth has known numerous eclipses before. In Exodus 10:21- 22; the Lord said to Moses; "Raise your hand towards the sky, and darkness thick enough to be felt will cover the land of Egypt. Moses raised his hands towards the sky, and there was total darkness throughout Egypt for three days."

Matthew 27:45 reports on another eclipse. "Now from the sixth hour there was darkness all the land unto the ninth hour."This was when Jesus Christ was crucified. I was told by my mother (Afua Amanuah) that in 1947, there was total darkness for some few hours in Ghana (then called Gold Coast) in West Africa. She said, Church bells were ringing and people (both pagans and Christians) ran to the Church. But this one seems to be something more, and not scheduled.

3. The Moon Became As Blood: The Bible does not say that the moon will be blood, but its color will be like blood.

4. The Stars Of Heaven Fall Unto The Earth: There will be showers of stars, meteorites, objects from the sky and will mark the dissolution of the world.

5. The Heaven Departed As A Scroll: This does not mean that the heaven passes out of existence any more.

6. Every Mountain And Island Were Moved Out Of Their Places: The mountains could not be found and every island disappeared. I believe this was for the preparation of the millennial on earth.

7. The Great Day Of His Wrath Is Come:

This *Great* Day of His wrath is different from that of Romans 2:5 and 16.This great day of His wrath will come during the lesser tribulation of three and a half years of Daniel's Seventieth Week. It is not the final judgment. The one in Romans 2: 5 and 16 refers to the final judgment which Revelation 20 also talks about.

The sixth seal- Anarchy

Between The Sixth And Seventh Seals:

The Sealing Of God's Servants(Revelation. 7:1- 8)

John said, he saw four angels standing at the four corners of the earth; holding back the four winds so that no wind should blow on the earth or the sea or against any tree (Revelation 7: 1).

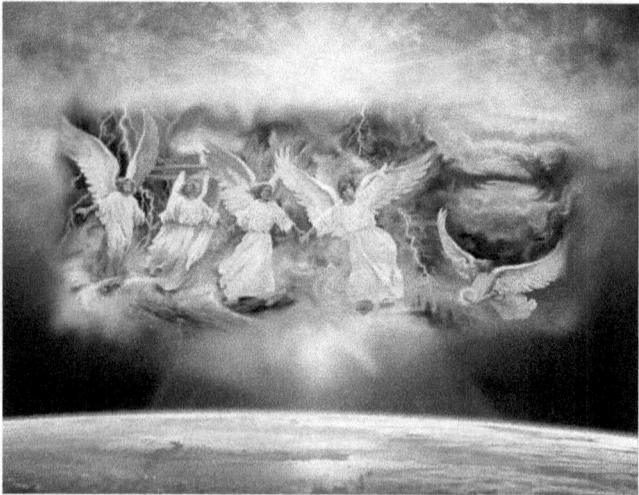

The Four Angels

These four angels are good angels whose duty

is to control all the winds of the earth, and not to allow any wind to blow against the land, the sea or against any tree. John said, he saw another angel coming up from the east with instruction for the four angels whom God had restrained until they mark the servants of God with a seal on their foreheads.(Revelation 7:2, 3). The seal here is a sign of protection for the saints in the time of the tribulation. With the seal there will be no destruction that can come to them. Even if they die, they have their place in heaven.

The One Hundred And Forty-Four Thousand (144,000)- Revelations 7:4-8

"And I heard a number of them which were sealed: and there were sealed an Hundred and Forty and Four Thousand of all the tribes of the children of Israel.

Of the tribe of Judah were sealed twelve thousand. Of the tribe of Reuben were sealed twelve thousand. Of the tribe of Gad were sealed twelve thousand. Of the tribe of Aser were sealed twelve thousand. Of the tribe of Napthalin were sealed twelve thousand. Of the tribe of Manasseh were sealed twelve thousand. Of the tribe of Simeon were sealed twelve thousand. Of the tribe of Levi were sealed twelve thousand. Of the tribe of Issachar were sealed twelve thousand. Of the tribe of Zebulon were sealed twelve thousand. Of the tribe of Joseph were sealed twelve thousand. Of the tribe of Benjamin were sealed twelve thousand.

Revelation 7:4-8

John said he heard the number of those who were sealed in all the tribes of the Children of Israel (JACOBS). These 144000 sealed refer to only Jacob's descendants. The twelve tribes of

Israel came as a result of Jacob's twelve children (Genesis 35:22-26).

After these twelve biological sons Jacob adopted Joseph's two sons, Ephraim and Manasseh "And now thy son Ephraim and Manasseh which were born into thee in the land of Egypt before I came into Egypt are mine; as Ruben and Simon, they shall be mine" *Genesis 48:5.*

When you compare Genesis 35:22 -26 with Revelation 7:4-8, you will realize that one of Jacob's biological sons, Dan was omitted and Manasseh, Joseph's son was added to replace Dan. The 144,000 therefore are all the tribes of children of Israel who were not saved when the rapture took place. These things took place between the sixth and seventh seals.

Identification Of The Four Kingdoms The Great Multitude: (Revelation 7:9-17)

".After this I beheld, and, lo, a great multitude, which no man could number, of all nations, and kindred, and people, and tongues, stood before the throne, and before the Lamb, clothed with white robes, and palms in their hands; And cried with a loud voice, saying, Salvation to our God which sitteth upon the throne, and unto the Lamb.

And all the angels stood round about the throne, and *about* the elders and the four beasts, and fell before the throne on their faces, and worshipped God, Saying, Amen: Blessing, and glory, and wisdom, and thanksgiving, and honor, and power, and might, be unto our God for ever and ever. Amen.

And one of the elders answered, saying unto me, what are these which are arrayed in white robes? And whence came they? And I said unto him, Sir, thou knowest. And he said to me, These are they which came out of great tribulation, and have washed their robes, and made them white in the blood of the Lamb.

Therefore are they before the throne of God, and serve him day and night in his temple: and he that sitteth on the throne shall dwell among them.

They shall hunger no more, neither thirst anymore; neither shall the sun light on them, nor any heat. For the lamb which is in the midst of the throne shall feed them, and shall lead them unto living fountains of waters: and God shall wipe away all tears from their eyes." *Revelation 7:9-17.*

John saw a crowd so large that it would be difficult even to estimate its size (Great Multitude). These people (Great Multitude) are the martyrs of the tribulation. Between the Sixth and Seventh Seals, John saw two separate groups, the 144,000 and the great multitude. The 144,000 are the elects of Israel. They were sealed against the great tribulation on earth while the Great Multitude are people from all nations, race, and language. They are those who came out of the great tribulation and have washed their robes in the blood of the Lamb. These people were before the throne. The great multitude has palms in their hands and songs on their lips. It is the sign of victory.

THE SEVENTH SEAL: Silence

"And when he had opened the seventh seal, there was silence in heaven about the space: of half an hour." *Revelation 8: 1*

There was a profound silence in heaven during

the thirty-minute interlude between the opening of the seals and the sounding of the trumpets. This was the separation between the Lesser Tribulation and Greater Tribulation, which was about to begin.

CHAPTER FIVE

HALF OF TRIBULATION WEEK

SEVEN ANGELS WITH SEVEN TRUMPETS

"And I saw the seven angels which stood before God; and to them were given seven trumpets. And another angel came and stood at the altar, having a golden censer; and there was given unto him much incense, that he should offer *it* with the prayers of all saints upon the golden altar which was before the throne.

And the smoke of the incense, which came with the prayers of the saints, ascended up before God out of the angel's hand. And the angel took the -censer, and filled it with fire of the altar, and cast *it* into the earth: and there were voices, and thunderings, and lightnings, and an earthquake. And the seven angels which had the seven trumpets prepared themselves to sound."- Revelation 8:2-6.

Referee Angels

John the Apostle describes what he saw out of the Seventh Seal. He saw seven angels with seven trumpets ready to sound. And God had arranged that whenever one of the angels blew the trumpet something peculiar followed immediately. One of the simplest ways to look at the *sounding of the* trumpet is to compare the trumpet to the whistle a referee uses in a game. During a football match or a basketball game, a referee is needed to regulate the match and give the cue to show whose turn it is to do what. Similarly, the angels with the trumpets can simply be referred to as umpires with trumpets. So that when the first angel blows the trumpet, then a series of things happen.

The blowing of the second trumpet also means the end of the first series of things and the, beginning of another. But before the trumpets could sound, there was an interlude. Another angel came and stood at the altar of incense with a golden incense burner. In the earthly tabernacle, which was made by Moses, the Altar of Incense occupied the middle space just before the inner veil in the Holy Place. Only one thing, sweet -smelling incense was allowed to be burned on this altar. No forbidden incense, animal-offering, grain-offering, wine-offering were allowed to be offered or burned on it.

Jesus, The Great High Priest

The High Priest was the only person assigned to bum incense on behalf of God's people. He alone could go to the place where the presence of God was and burn the incense. John said, the Altar of Incense [The Golden Altar] was in Heaven and was situated before the throne. And another angel, with a golden incense-burner came and stood at the altar. Since only the high priest could offer the incense, therefore this other angel is the Lord Jesus Christ, in His present ministry as our great High Priest. "Seeing then that we have a great high priest that is passed into the heavens, Jesus the Son of God, let us hold fast *our* profession." *Hebrews 4:14* The word *great* here speaks of the dignity and Person of Christ.

His peculiar sacrifice and the place where He now officiates (Heaven) set him apart from all the other high priests. His priesthood is forever and He is making other priests unto God. He is Jesus, the Son of God. Jesus stands for Savior. But by nature He is equal to God.

We are not talking about a man and a Mediator, but God's own Son representing us. And this qualifies Him as the Great High Priest of the Church. The Son of God has done the greatest part of His work as priest. Now He is doing the rest through intercession for the saints. Therefore, what John saw was Christ doing His present ministry of holding up Believers prayers to God. The thundering, and lightning were the answers God gave to the prayers of the saints. Christians who limit God in their lives should take a second look at the effect of their prayers offered through Christ. When you pray, the enemy hears these frightful thunders and lightning and yet we perceive ourselves as powerless. The earthquake is a token of the

Lord's judgment to the world. And this is an evidence of His power, majesty and glory.

CHAPTER SIX

TRUMPET

FIRST TRUMPET: Hail-Fire And Blood

"The first angel sounded, and there followed hail and fire mingled with blood, and they were cast upon the earth: and the third part of trees was burnt up, and all green grass were burnt up" *Revelation 8:7*

When the first trumpet sounded, hail and fire mixed with blood followed. These three things represent a terrible destruction on earth. And during that time it will affect one-third vegetation of the earth. This implies that agriculture would be adversely affected. The result could be famine.

First Trumpet: Hail-Fire And Blood

SECOND TRUMPET: Sea To Blood

"And the second angel sounded, and as it were a great mountain burning with fire was cast into the sea: and the third part of the sea became blood; And the third part of the creatures which were in the sea, and had life, died; and the third part of the ships were destroyed" *Revelation 8:8&9*

The difference between the first and the second trumpet is that whereas the first trumpet involved earth, the judgment of the second trumpet was upon the sea. This time one third of the sea turned into blood, one third of the living creatures in the sea died and another third of the ships were, which means it will be difficult to work or travel on the sea.

SECOND TRUMPET-THIRD PART OF THE SEA BECAME BLOOD

THIRD TRUMPET: **Bitter Waters**

And the third angel sounded, and there fell a great star from heaven, burning as it were a lamp, and it fell upon the third part of the rivers and upon the fountains of waters; And the name of the star is called Wormwood: and the third part of the waters became Wormwood; and many died of the waters, because they were made: bitter" *Revelation* 8:IO&II

The third trumpet was a judgment, which affected fresh water supply. John said, a large star, burning like a lamp, dropped from the sky and fell upon one-third of rivers and fountains of waters. One third of the waters turned bitter as a result of the star called Wormwood that fell upon the rivers and upon the fountains of waters.

THIRD TRUMPET-BITTER WATERS

According to the New Unger's Bible dictionary by Marrill F. Unger, Wormwood is a bitter plant in waste places; usually in the desert. It can be found in the deserts of Palestine and Syria. During Jeremiah's time, Israel forsook God and went after other gods and Jehovah in His wrath revealed that He would feed them with wormwood.

"And the Lord saith, because they have forsaken my law which I set before them, and have not obeyed my voice, neither walked therein; But have walked after the imagination of their own heart, and after Baalim, which their fathers taught them: Therefore thus saith the Lord of hosts, the God of Israel; Behold, I will feed them, even this people, with WORMWOOD, and give them water of gall to drink" *Jeremiah 9:13-15.*

FOURTH TRUMPET: **Planet Darkened**

"And the fourth angel sounded, and the third part of the sun was smitten, and the third part of the moon, and the third part of the stars, so as the third part of them was darkened, and the day shone not for a third part of it, and the night likewise" Revelation 8:12

The Planets (sun, moon and stars) are affected by the judgment as a result of the blowing of the fourth trumpet. One third of the sun was struck, and one third of the moon and stars lost their power of brightness; there was no light for three days and three nights. Many heinous crimes are committed under the cover of darkness. Thus when the day becomes dark as the night, it means there could be an upsurge of evil.

Cry Of An Eagle

"And I beheld, and heard an angel flying through the midst of heaven, saying with a loud voice, Woe, Woe, Woe, to the inhabitants of the earth by reason of the other voices of the trumpet of the three angels which are yet to sound!"-*Revelation 8:13.*

Some manuscripts translate this flying angel as an "eagle", as in Deuteronomy 28:49. "The Lord shall bring a nation against thee from far, from the end of the earth, as swift as the eagle flieth; a nation whose tongue thou shalt not *understand ;"Deuteronomy 28:49*

Here, we notice that the seven-trumpet series is divided into two events, similar to what happened under the sixth seal. The eagle that was flying in the midst of heaven delivered a message. The message was an announcement of three Woe's to the inhabitants of the earth signifying the three trumpets of woes about to be sounded. It would be horrible *for* all who would be living on earth when the trumpets sound.

**FOURTH TRUMPET-PLANET DARKENED &
CRY OF AN EAGLE**

CHAPTER SEVEN

TRUMPETS OF WOES

FIFTH TRUMPET: First Woe

"And the fifth angel sounded, and I saw a star fall from heaven unto earth: and to him was given the key of the bottomless pit. And he opened the bottomless pit, and there arose a smoke out of the pit, as the smoke of a great furnace: and the sun and the air were darkened by reason of the smoke of the pit. And there came out of the smoke locusts upon the earth: and unto them was given power, as the scorpions of the earth have power.

And it was commanded them that they should not hurt the grass of the earth, neither any green thing, neither any tree; but only those men which have not the seal of God on their foreheads. And to them it was given that they should not kill them, but that they should be tormented five months: and their torment was as the torment of a scorpion, when he striketh a man. And in those days shall men seek death, and shall not find it; and shall desire to die, and death shall flee from them and the shapes of the locusts were like unto horses prepared unto battle; and on their heads were as it were crowns like gold, and their faces were as the faces *of* men. And they have hair of women, and their teeth were as their teeth of Lions, And they had breastplates, as it were breastplates of iron; and the sound of chariots *of* many horses running to battle. And they had tails like unto scorpions, and there were stings in their tails and their power was to hurt men five months. And they had a king over them, which is the angel of the bottomless pit, whose name in the Hebrews tongue is Abaddon, but in the Greek tongue had his name Appollyon (Revelation 9:1-11).

There are five things to be observed here, which are: Star, Key, Bottomless Pit or Abyss, Locusts and Abaddon or Appollyon. When the fifth angel blew his trumpet, John said he saw a star that had fallen down to earth, and it was given the key to the abyss.

FIFTH TRUMPET-1ST WOE

Custodian Of Abyss

This star is the angel who is the custodian of the bottomless pit. Some understand this star to be an evil agent (fallen angel) or Satan. But there is a big problem with this line of thinking. It seems unreasonable for God to trust an evil angel or Satan with the key of the bottomless pit. This is the same angelic personage that binds Satan at the beginning of the millennium (Revelation 20: 1-3).

Further this angel is not Abaddon (Apollyon), because Abaddon is an evil agent of Satan and the king of the demons in the Abyss. The key that was given to the angel fallen from heaven is the key for the prison house of the demons [the bottomless pit]. How can God trust an evil angel or Satan with this key?

Another thing to note is that this prison house of the demons or the bottomless pit is not hell or hades. This is the prison of evil spirits, where Satan and all the fallen angels will be bound for 1000 years. In Luke's gospel some demons described it as the deep. The legion of demons in the mad man of Gadarenes begged Jesus not to send them there. And they besought him that he would not command them to go out into the deep." *Luke* 8:31 The word deep here is the same as Abyss or The Bottomless Pit.

John said, the angel who was given the key then opened The Bottomless Pit and smoke poured out of it. This smoke was compared to the smoke from a large furnace. It darkened the sunlight and the airwaves. And locusts came down out of the smoke upon the earth, and they were given the same kind of power that scorpions have. These locusts represent demons. They are not ordinary locusts. These demon locusts have been commanded not to hurt the grass, herbs and trees, but their target is to torment only human beings. Their power works on people who do not have the seal of God on their foreheads. Moreover, these demon locusts have been given the sting of scorpions. They would torment them for five months. During these months men will seek death, but will not find it. This means that they will want to die, but death will flee from them. The Apostle also described these demonic locusts. He said they looked like horses ready for battle; and they wore something like crowns of gold, and their faces were like men's faces. But their hair was like women's hair their teeth like lion's teeth, their chests were covered with what looked like iron breastplates, and their wings made sounds like the noise of chariots rushing into battle.

Moreover, these locusts had a king. But ordinary locusts have no king. According to Proverbs 30:27, the locusts have no king, yet go they forth all of them by bands. The name of the king of these demon locusts was mentioned as Abaddon in Hebrews tongue or Apollyon in Greek tongue. It is also a fallen angel who was in the abyss with them and will come out with them as their leader.

SIXTH TRUMPET: **Second Woe**

"And the sixth angel sounded, and I heard a voice from the four horns of the golden altar which is before God. Saying to the sixth angels which had the trumpet, loose the four angels which are bound in the great river Euphrates.

And the four angels were loosed, *which* were prepared for an hour and a day, and a month, and a year, for to slay the third part of men. And the number of the army of the horsemen was two hundred thousand -thousand and I heard the number of them.

And thus I saw the horses in the vision, and them that sat on them, having breastplates of fire, and jacinth, and brimstone: and the heads of the horses were as the heads of lions; and out of their mouths issued fire and smoke and brimstone. By these three was the third part of men killed, by the fire, and by the smoke, and the brimstone which issued out of their mouths. For their power is in their mouth, and in their tails: for their tails were like unto serpents, and had heads, and with them they do hurt.

And the rest of the men which were not killed by these plagues yet repented not of the works of their hands, that they should not worship devils, and idols of gold, and silver and brass, and stone, and of wood: which neither can see, nor hear, nor walk: Neither repented they of their murders, nor of their sorceries, nor of their fornications, nor of their thefts." *Revelation 9:13-21.*

When the sixth angel blew his trumpet, John said he heard a voice coming from the four corners of the golden altar standing before God. The voice said to the sixth angel, release the four angels who are bound at the great Euphrates River.

It seems John is describing two kinds of demons, which will invade the earth during the tribulation. The fifth trumpet brought in the locust demons but the sixth trumpet ushers in the second invasion.

The four special satanic angels were released for a fixed time - an hour, a day, a month and a year. Some refer to it as thirteen months. The damage by this invasion was to slay one third of humanity. John said he heard the number of the armies of this invasion (the horsemen) were two hundred million. The description of these demons, unlike the first invasion" seems to be some type of hellish horse.

John said the breastplates of the horses and their riders were fiery red as fire, dark blue as jacinth or sapphire, and yellow as brimstone or sulphur. Then the heads of the horses were as the head of lions; and from their mouths came out fire, smoke and brimstone.

The power of their horses is in their mouths and also in their tails. Their tails are like snakes with heads, and they use them to hurt people. This invasion is therefore the opposite of the fifth trumpet invasion during which no man was able to die even though they want to. These horsemen are released to kill men while the locusts merely torment. What happened to the rest who were not killed by these plagues? John said they did not turn away from what they themselves had made. They did not stop worshipping demons, nor the idols of gold, silver, bronze, stone, and wood, which cannot see, hear, and walk. Moreover, they did not repent of their murders, their magics, their sexual immorality or their stealing. Do you know that even today in the face of the most fearsome predictions of the destruction of the world in newspapers and television, sinners stubbornly refuse to repent? This is the world we live in. It is a world that resists God to the bitter end. They prefer to make their own gods, than to obey God.

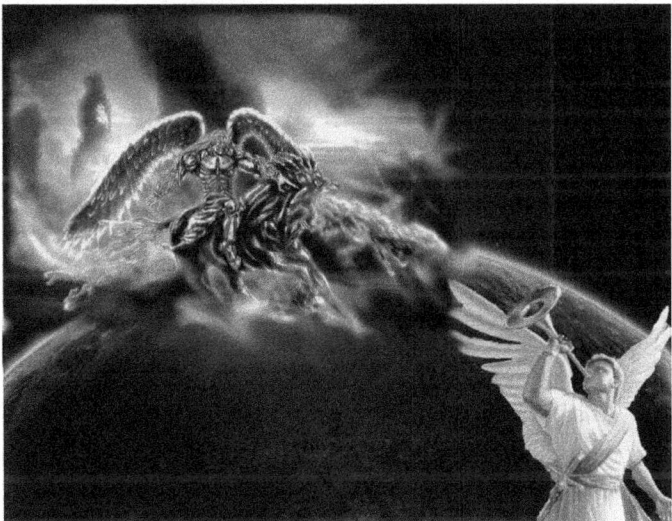

SIXTH TRUMPET-2ND WOE

The Mighty Angel And Little Scroll

And I saw another mighty angel come down from heaven, clothed with a cloud: and a rainbow was upon his head, and his face was as it were the sun, and his feet as pillars of fire: And he had in his hand a little book open: and he set his right foot upon the sea, and his left foot on the earth. And cried with a loud voice, as when a lion roareth: and when he had cried, seven thunders uttered their voices.

And when the seven thunders uttered their voices, I was about to write: and I heard a voice from heaven saying unto me, seal up those things which the seven thunders uttered their voices, and write them not.

And the angel which 1 saw stand upon the sea and upon the earth lifted up his hand to heaven. And swore by Him that liveth for ever and ever, who created heaven and the earth, and the things that therein are, and the earth, and the things that therein are, and the sea, and the things which are therein, that there should be time no longer: But in the days of the voices of the seventh angel, when he shall begin to sound, the mystery of God, should be finished, as he hath declared to his servants the prophets' Revelation 10:1-7.

There is a time-out period between the sixth and the seventh trumpets. This period follows the same pattern as there was between the six and seventh seals. During this break two significant events took place.

1. The Measuring of The Temple of God

2. The Two Witnesses

The identity of the mighty angel is no doubt Christ. Some writers refer or write about this mighty angel here as Michael the Archangel. There is something peculiar about this angel from those sounding the trumpets. This angel here is an angel who symbolizes Christ.

He reflects His glory and bears a distinguishing sign of Christ Himself (Revelation 4:3).

Notice that He was clothed with a cloud: Clouds are referred to as showing the power and wisdom of God. According to Isaiah 19: 1 the Lord rides upon a swift cloud. Jehovah God told Moses, "Lo, I come unto thee in a thick cloud..." (Exodus 19:9).

During Jesus transfiguration, a cloud covered Him. "While he yet spoke, behold, a bright cloud overshadowed them; and behold a voice out of the cloud., which said, this is my beloved Son, in whom I am well pleased: hear ye him".*Matthew 17:5*

A cloud played a role in Jesus' ascension. And when he had spoken these things, while they behold, he was taken up; and a cloud received him out of their sight" *Acts* 1:9

Moreover, this mighty angel spoke about the two witnesses as "my *two* witnesses" (Revelation 11::3). Only God is capable of addressing angels as His. *Rainbow is* never used in the Bible apart from describing the presence of God. John described the throne set in heaven, and one sat on the throne with a rainbow round about the throne (Revelation 4:3).

Ezekiel 1:28 also says about his vision of God; Like the appearance of a rainbow in the clouds on a rainy day, so was the radiance around him. This angel reflects the glory of Christ Himself. The fact that He set His right foot upon the sea, and His left foot on earth shows Christ's right to claim the earth as His own. "The sea is his, and he made it: and his hands formed the dry land" (Psalm 95:5).

The angel's loud voice, and the seven thunders give full testimony of Christ's authority exhibited over the earth by this angel. Joel said; The Lord roars from Mount Zion; his voice thunders from Jerusalem; and the earth and the sky tremble (Joel 3: 16). This angel took a vow in the name of God that "There should be time no longer" or 'Time has run out". Shows Christ's divine sovereignty and control in these matters of judgment. Let me make myself clear here; Christ's presence on earth during the sixth and seventh trumpets is not His formal possession on earth. Neither, these statements refers to God's possession of the earth in the middle of the week.

The expression, "There will be no more delay!" refers to the Mystery of God immediate fulfillment because it is a previously hidden truth now to be revealed in the next verse which focuses upon Christ, in whom God's plan for earth is centered and unfolded.

John And The Little Book Revelation 10:8-11

"And the voice which I heard from heaven spake unto me again, and said, Go, Go and take the little book which is open in the hand of the angel which standeth upon the sea and upon the earth. And I went unto the angel, and said unto him, Give me the little book. And he said unto me, Take it and eat it up and it shall make honey. And I took the little book out of the angel's hand, and ate it up; and it was in my mouth sweet as honey and as soon as I had eaten it, my belly was bitter. And he said unto me "thou must prophesy again before many peoples, and nations, and tongues and Kings." Revelation 10:8-11

John's encounter with this mighty angel added another aspect to this revelation. Seven thunders uttered their voices and John was about to write.

But he heard a voice instructing him to seal them up and not to write it. The same voice told him to open the scroll or the little book. (Compare this with Daniel 12:4, 9). Then the angel told him to eat it and that it will turn sour in his stomach but sweet as honey in his mouth. The gospel is good *news,* and it is sweet as honey to our taste because of the salvation it brings. However, when we quantify the number of individuals who are lost and continue in rebellion against God it brings pain to our stomachs. After he ate the scroll he was told to prophesy. This had a drastic effect on John's ministry as a seer. Through the record of this revelation this Apostle has continued to make impart on every generation.

He has made known the message of God to everyone who reads the Bible. Therefore, he has proclaimed God's message to many nations, races, languages, and Kings.

Temple Measured

"And there was given me reeds like unto a rod: and the angel stood, saying, Rise, and measure the temple of God, and the altar, them that worship therein. But the court which is without the temple leave out, and measure it not; for it is given unto the Gentiles: and the holy city shall they tread under foot forty and two months." Revelation 11:1, 2.

John is put to work here with a reed like a rod, as the measuring instrument to measure the Temple. This shows again the Lord's dealing with the Jews and their 'worship in a restored temple in Jerusalem, "The Holy City". This temple is not the millennial temple. Here, John is to measure the temple and the altar, and to record the identity of its worshippers.

However, the outer court that was in the possession of the Gentiles was not measured. Which means the outer court is to be cast out. Not only will the outer court be given to the Gentiles to be trodden down, but the holy city itself will be trodden down also for *forty--two* months.

This is in confirmation of what Jesus said in Luke 21:24; "And they shall fall by the edge of the sword, and shall be led away captive into all nations: and Jerusalem shall be trodden down of the Gentiles, until the times of the Gentiles be fulfilled."

CHAPTER EIGHT

THE TWO WITNESSES

And I will give unto my two Witnesses, and they shall prophesy a thousand two hundred and threescore days, clothed in sackcloth. These are the olive trees, and two candlesticks standing before the God of the earth. And if any man will hurt them, fire proceedeth out of their mouth, and devoureth their enemies: and if any man will hurt them, he must in this manner be killed. These have power to shut heaven, that it rain not in the days of their prophecy: and have power over waters to turn them to blood, and to smite the earth with all plagues, as often as they will. And when they shall have finished their testimony, the beast that ascended out of the bottomless pit shall make war against them and shall overcome them, and kill them. And their dead bodies shall lie in the street of the great city, which spiritually is called Sodom and Egypt, where also our lord was crucified.

And they of the people and kindred's and tongues and nations shall see their dead bodies three days, and half, and shall not suffer their dead bodies to be put in graves. And they that: dwell upon the earth shall rejoice over them, and make merry, and shall send gifts one to another; because these two prophets tormented them that dwelt on the earth. And after three days and an half the Spirit of Life from God entered into them, and they stood upon their feet; and great fear fell upon them which saw them. And they heard a great voice from heaven saying unto them, come up hither.

And they ascended up to heaven in a cloud; and their enemies beheld them. And the same hour was there a great earthquake, and the tenth part of the city fell and in the earthquake were slain of men seven thousand: and the remnant were affrighted, and gave glory to the God of heaven." *Revelation 11:3-13*

The big and interesting question that has been debated over and over is, who are these witnesses?" They are commonly identified as Moses and Elijah; Moses and Enoch or Elijah and Enoch. Let us take these three men one by one and look at their lives so we could more accurately suggest who they are.

Moses

Some hold that in Exodus 7: 19, 20 Moses commanded Aaron to take his stick and hold it out over all the rivers, canals, and pools in

Egypt. Scriptures record that all the rivers turned into blood and this will be repeated by one of the witnesses during the tribulation so Moses is suggested as one of the two witnesses. Moreover, Moses appeared with Elijah on the Mount of Transfiguration (Matthew 17:3).

Elijah

Some also think that Elijah prevented rain for three years and six months (1 Kings 17: 1, James 5:17) and this will be repeated by one of the witnesses during the tribulation. During the contest with the worshippers of Baal, Elijah called Fire to come down from heaven to consume his sacrifice (2 Kings 1: 10). Calling down fire is part of the agenda of the witnesses. Elijah was taken up to Heaven by a chariot of fire pulled by horses of fire so he did not die (2Kings 2: 11). Again Elijah appeared with Moses on the Mount of Transfiguration (Matthew 17:3). Out of the lot, Elijah's credentials seem to fit the part most.

Enoch

The only thing we can say about Enoch is that he walked with God and as a reward of his sanctity he was transported into heaven without dying" (Genesis 5:22; Hebrews 11:5).

Death of Moses

Many believe that Moses and Elijah have more explicit association or have exercised the same miraculous powers like the two witnesses, and therefore they fit the description.

However, I refute this statement because they are out of harmony with scripture. Revelation 11:3 says, "And I will give power unto my two witnesses..." Thus they are not powerful in themselves. It is the Lord who will give them the anointing for His work.

Hebrews 9:27, nullified the Moses theory "And as it is appointed unto men once to die, but after this the judgment." Revelation 11:7 further deepens the error"...the beast that ascended out of the bottomless pit shall make war against them, and shall overcome them, and kill them." When we take these two scriptures in account, we can say that Moses could not be one of the two witnesses because he experienced physical death.

"So Moses the servant of the Lord died there in the land of Moab, according to the word of the Lord. And he buried him in a valley in the land of Moab, over against Beth-peor: but no man knoweth of his sepulcher unto this day. Deuteronomy 34:5&6 Moses will have a resurrected body and a resurrected body can never die physically or be killed. Therefore, I believe that it is Enoch and Elijah who are the two witnesses, since: these two men are the only two people in scripture who did not experience physical death. They will be sent back to the earth as witnesses and will eventually die a martyr's death.

The Two Witnesses

Nature of Their Work

The length or period for them to prophesy will be forty-two months or 1,260 days. During the same time the Antichrist will reign supreme (the last three and a half years of the great tribulation, (42 months at 30 days to a month is 1,260 days). The two witnesses will dress in sackcloth as a symbol of mourning, because they identify themselves with Israel's grievous sins and Jerusalem's, wickedness. They will also receive power and support from the Lord. John described them as the two olive trees and two candlesticks" (Revelation 11:4).

This same phrase appears in the Old Testament. "...These are the two anointed ones, that stand by the Lord of whole earth." **Zechariah 4:2, 3,11 &14.** In short, the Lord has made them olive-trees and lamps that stand before Him, so that there "Will be oil always in their lamps for the period of 1,260 days. If anyone tries to harm them, fire will come out of their mouths to destroy that person. This power is their security and defense for them to witness or prophesy. With the power and support by the Lord, they can shut up heaven so that there will be no rain during the time of their prophecy. They have power over waters to turn it into blood, and also to strike the earth with all kinds of plague as often as they will. When they finish their testimony, God will permit the beast to come from the abyss (the bottomless pit) to attack them, and kill them. Their bodies will lie in the open street of the great city of Jerusalem, which is spiritually called Sodom for monstrous and unusual wickedness. People from all nations, tribes, languages, and races will look at their bodies for three and a half days and will refuse them to be buried.

The anti-Christian world will gloat over their bodies and will celebrate and send presents to each other, because these two witnesses had tormented their consciences.

The Two Witnesses Killed

Resurrection of Witnesses

After three and a half days, the breath of life from God will enter into them and they will stand upon their feet. Isn't that wonderful? God will not only put life, but also put courage into them, to stand upon their feet, and ascend into heaven before the eyes of their enemies. This will produce terror upon their enemies. After this there will be a violent earthquake and a tenth of the enemy (Jerusalem) will be destroyed. Seven thousand people will be killed in the earthquake and survivors will be terrified. The fear of God will fall upon them, and they will give glory to the God of Heaven and recognize Jesus as Lord.

Two Witnesses Resurrected

CHAPTER NINE

FINAL BLAST

Seventh Trumpet: **Third Woe**

"And the seventh angel sounded; and there were great voices in heaven, saying, The kingdoms of this world are become the kingdoms of our Lord, and of his Christ; and he shall reign for ever and ever. And the four and twenty elders, which sat before God on their seats, fell upon their faces, and worshipped God, 'Saying, We give thee thanks, 0 Lord God Almighty, which art, and wast, and art to come; because thou hast taken to thee thy great power, and hast reigned.

And the nations were angry, and thy wrath is come, and the time of the dead, that they should be judged, and that thou shouldest give reward unto thy servants the prophets, and to the saints, and them that fear thy name, small and great; and shouldest destroy them which destroy the earth.

And the temple of God was opened in heaven, and there was seen in his temple the ark of his testament: and there were lightnings, and voices, and thunderings, and an earthquake, and great hail." Revelation 11:15-19.

The sounding of the seventh trumpet mark the beginning of the second part of the three and a half years (the midst of the week) the great tribulation. This time can be explained as the space between the Little Book when it was opened, the Temple Measurement and the Two witnesses. These events form the first part of the three and a half years (lesser tribulation).

But the second part of the three and a half years {the great tribulation) caused the suspension of the sounding of the seventh trumpet. John needed to observe the intervening occurrences for the records. Then John said, he saw the seventh angel blow his trumpet, and there were loud voices of the saints and angels in heaven saying that the Kingdoms of this world have become the kingdoms of our Lord, Jesus Christ (Revelation 11:15). This means that the power to rule over the world now belongs to our lord and His Anointed one and his reign shall never end. Then the twenty-four elders, who sit on their thrones before God, fell upon their faces and worshipped God, saying: We thank you,

Lord God Almighty the one who is and was, because you have taken your great power and have begun to rule. The heathen were angry, because the time for their wrath has come. And it was time for God to take revenge upon the enemies of his people, just to recompense tribulation to those who had troubled the earth. What happened here under the seventh trumpet does not indicate that God becomes absolute ruler over the world. This is not the eschatological Kingdom (the study of God and religious truth that treats death, resurrection, immortality, the end *of* the world and final judgment.)

I believe the judgment *of* the dead, recompensing tribulation *to* those who had troubled the earth and rewarding the faithful servants both small and great will be fulfilled in their own time. The reason being this, Jesus talked about separation of the sheep and the goats in the gospels. When the Son of man shall come in his glory and all the holy angels with him, then shall he sit upon the throne of his glory. And before him shall be gathered all nations: and he shall separate them one from another, as a shepherd divideth his sheep from goats." Matthew 25:31-32. Paul also says; "For we must all appear before the judgment seat a/Christ; that every one may receive the things done in his body, according to that he hath done, whether it be good or bad." 2 Corinthians 5:10. John himself talks about the final judgment where the dead will be judged in Revelation 20: 11-15

The seventh trumpet closes with another consequence. This time John saw the temple of God opened in heaven and within this temple was the Ark of His Testament. Some writers say that this Ark of the Testament is the same ark

Moses made. But I believe Moses own was a pattern of what John saw in heaven. The good news about this Ark is that it is the sign of the presence of God returning to His people. When God returns to His people it is cause for celebration. Life without God is death. God is like breath for every creature. In Him we live, move and have our being. The fearful things that would happen during these times should cause the reader to pause and think. I will give everything on earth to escape such Judgment. Anybody who wants to escape this judgment should first judge himself.

SEVENTH TRUMPET-3ᴿᴰ WOE

Where do you stand with God? What have you done with the offer of His only Begotten Son? Is He still Lord of your life? Have you talked to Him today? Did you hear His voice today? The only route out of this judgment is to accept Jesus as your Lord and personal Savior.

As I wrap up this teaching, I wish to help you get on track with the Lord.

If you want to accept Jesus as your personal Savior and Lord, then say this prayer with meaning, as your own.

Dear Lord, I am a sinner and I cannot save myself. Please forgive me for my sins. Wash me in your blood. I believe that you died for my sins on Calvary and on the third day you rose from the dead. Come and live, in my heart and be my Lord Forever. Thank you Jesus for receiving me. Amen.

For further enquiries about your salvation or the next part of this book please write to:

REV. DR. FRED OPOKU-GYIMAH,

Pentecostal Redeemer's Temple
1537-41 Bergen Avenue Brooklyn,
New York 11213

ABOUT THE AUTHOR

Apostle Dr. Fred Opoku-Gyimah is the General Overseer of Born Again Believer's Ministries (BAB), Charismatic Praise Ministries all in Ghana W/A and Pentecostal Redeemer's Temple Inc. Brooklyn NY. USA. He is also the Chancellor of Immanuel Bible Institute & Seminary in Brooklyn NY USA and Ghana Campus.

In September 28th 1979 he was called by the power of the risen Christ with a mandate to take the gospel to the nations with the dynamic inspiring and anointed Word of God! He is known for his remarkable teaching and deliverance Ministries, an International Motivational Conference Speaker and Marriage Counseling.

He is the author of The Hope of the Church (Rapture & Judgment); Unlocked Your Powers of Success and The Effective Leader. For 37 years' experience as a Pastor, he has been teaching on Spiritual Warfare, End Time Prophecy, Five-fold Ministry (Ascension Gifts), Church Management, Leadership, Understanding Your Potential, Potential Principles and Demonology. In fact, God has been using him in delivering many people out from Satanic attack/spiritualism (demonic & Cults) in Africa, United States, United Kingdom, Caribbean Islands and India.

Dr. Fred Opoku-Gyimah holds a bachelor Degree in Biblical Studies, Master of Arts in Christian Education and a Doctorate Degree in Divinity from Canon Bible College & Seminary – Orlando Florida. He also holds a Master of Religious Arts Degree in Theology and a Doctorate in Theology from Jacksonville Theological & Seminary Florida.